EDGE BOOKS

SPORTS TO THE EXTREME

EXTREME
Land Sports

BY ERIN K BUTLER

raintree
a Capstone company — publishers for children

Raintree is an imprint of Capstone Global Library Limited, a company incorporated in England and Wales having its registered office at 264 Banbury Road, Oxford, OX2 7DY – Registered company number: 6695582

www.raintree.co.uk
myorders@raintree.co.uk

Edited by Nikki Ramsay
Designed by Sara Radka
Production by Laura Manthe

ISBN 978-1-4747-4791-2 (library binding)
22 21 20 19 18 17
10 9 8 7 6 5 4 3 2 1

British Library Cataloguing in Publication Data
A full catalogue record for this book is available from the British Library.

Acknowledgements
iStockphoto: cover; Shutterstock: 1, 5, 6, 9, 23, 25, 26, 27; Newscom: Xinhua/Liang Xu, 6; Shutterstock: Jon Nicholls Photography, 11; Newscom: ZUMAPRESS/K.C. Alfred/San Diego Union-Tribune, 12; Shutterstock: Sergei Bachlakov, 15; Shutterstock: Vava Vladimir Jovanovic, 17; Shutterstock: homydesign, 19; Shutterstock: Frolova_Elena, 20; Getty Images, 29

Graphic elements by Book Buddy Media.

The publisher does not endorse products whose logos may appear on objects in images in this book.

Every effort has been made to contact copyright holders of material reproduced in this book. Any omissions will be rectified in subsequent printings if notice is given to the publisher.

All the Internet addresses (URLs) given in this book were valid at the time of going to press. However, due to the dynamic nature of the Internet, some addresses may have changed, or sites may have changed or ceased to exist since publication. While the author and publisher regret any inconvenience this may cause readers, no responsibility for any such changes can be accepted by either the author or the publisher.

Contents

Extreme land sports

You might be on a mountain. You might be on the road, in the desert or at a skatepark. It doesn't matter where you are – extreme sports can take place around the globe. A real expert can pull off amazing stunts anywhere on land.

Extreme sports are different to the regular sports you might see on TV. Extreme sports involve high speeds, thrilling jumps and lots of risk. In extreme land sports, competitors use the environment around them to push their bodies to the limit. They might climb over or leap from rock **formations**, roads or walls.

Extreme sports are especially popular with young people. They see extreme sports as a way to combine creativity and physical skill. The extreme sport community values each individual. Whether someone is shredding in a skatepark, exploring new geological areas or inventing tricks, they all add to the world of extreme sports.

EXTREME FACT!

More than 22 million people participate in extreme sports each year.

formation – the way in which items, such as rocks, are arranged

Mountainboarding allows people to tackle areas no boarder has ever explored.

Rock climbers try to travel light, but they need to bring all their equipment with them as they climb.

ROCK CLIMBING PRODIGY

Ashima Shiraishi is the world's best female rock cimber. Ashima started climbing when she was just six years old. Today she can climb difficult walls at lightning speed. In 2016, at the age of 15, Ashima became the first woman to complete a climb that was rated V15 – the most challenging rating. Ashima hopes to compete in rock climbing during the next Summer Olympic Games.

CHAPTER 1

Rock climbing

One of the most thrilling extreme land sports is rock climbing. This sport involves climbing over rocks, boulders and other obstacles to reach a **summit**. Long ago, this sport was simply a dangerous part of travelling. Climbing rocks was often necessary to get from one place to another. Over time, people began to enjoy climbing for fun.

But rock climbing comes with many risks, thanks to one unstoppable force – gravity. If climbers fall, they can be seriously hurt. Climbers love to face this risk and overcome danger.

Some people climb indoors on specially built rock walls. Others climb outside on natural rocks and mountains. Most of the time, people use a rope and harness for safety.

There are different methods climbers can use. Beginners use top-roping, which involves climbing with a partner. Lead/sport climbing focuses on the technique, not just the destination. Traditional climbers develop their own routes based on cracks in the rocks. Bouldering is a type of climbing done closer to the ground, and does not use a rope.

summit – the very top of a mountain; many summits are covered with snow

CHAPTER 2

Abseiling

Getting from a high point to a low point is a useful skill for many extreme sports, such as mountain climbing and snowboarding. Abseiling, also called rappelling, grew out of that need. As people continued developing abseiling techniques, it became a sport of its own.

In order to abseil, you need a rope, an anchor and a harness. A good rope, one that can hold the abseiler's weight, is the most essential part of climbing safety. The anchor is carefully attached to a high point. This could be the top of a cliff, a wall or another vertical surface. Then the abseiler loops the rope through a **friction device**. The rope gets attached to the abseiler's harness. Once everything is ready to go, the abseiler **descends**, bouncing off the wall with his or her feet while travelling towards the ground.

Once someone has become an experienced abseiler, he or she can begin using new techniques. This could mean abseiling head first, upside down, or even without a harness. Some extreme abseilers also try to descend as quickly as they can, adding an extra level of excitement and danger. The world record for a 100-metre (328-foot) abseil is 8.99 seconds.

friction device – a mechanical piece of equipment that helps control a rope

descend – to move from a higher place to a lower place

In addition to other safety gear, abseilers always wear helmets in case of falling rocks.

CHAPTER 3

Skateboarding

The earliest skateboards were used as far back as the early 1900s. People began experimenting at home by attaching wheels to boards. Then, around the 1960s, companies began to sell skateboards. Easy access to professionally made boards allowed the sport to become much more popular.

Skateboarding can be either a team sport or an individual sport. At its most basic level, skateboarding is simply a way to travel from one place to another. Riders stand on a wheeled board that is 71 to 81 centimetres (28 to 32 inches) long, and push themselves along using one foot. But when skateboarding goes extreme, it can be truly death-defying. Extreme skateboarding involves riders performing tricks, spins and jumps. Riders are always thinking of new, creative ways to use their boards.

There are two main types of extreme skateboarding – vertical and street-style. Vertical, or vert, skateboarding is when riders skate on a halfpipe. A halfpipe is a ramp shaped like the letter U. By using these ramps, skaters can fly into the air on their boards and perform tricks. In street-style skating, riders perform tricks on stairs, rails and other obstacles.

At skateparks like those in Venice Beach, California, USA, skateboarders get to practice tricks and show off their moves. They also learn from other boarders.

Tony Hawk competed in pro skateboarding for 17 years. He retired after performing a 900-degree turn in the X Games.

Skateboarders can show off their skills in competitions. The most famous are the X Games and World Cup Skateboarding. Skateboarders from all over the world travel to perform their best stunts. One of the all-time best skateboarders is Tony Hawk, who has won more than 70 skateboarding competitions.

The X Games showcases both summer and winter sports, including bicycle motocross (BMX), motocross, snowboarding and, of course, skateboarding. Both men and women can compete in street, vert and park events. Since the X Games moves to different locations around the world, skateboarders get to show off in new environments.

World Cup Skateboarding was developed in 1993 and the first competition was held a year later. This world tour focuses on professional skateboarders. Today World Cup Skateboarding has more than 10 events. Just like in the X Games, both men and women can compete.

EXTREME FACT!

There are more than 1,250 skateparks in the United Kingdom.

One special branch of skateboarding is called longboarding. A longboard is exactly what it sounds like – a longer version of a skateboard. Longboards are typically at least 91 cm (36 inches) long, but some are as long as 152 cm (60 inches). They can also be wider than regular skateboards.

Longboards are generally easier to ride than skateboards. Their length allows riders to balance more easily. Unlike skateboards, longboards are designed for long-distance travel.

There are four main styles of riding a longboard: cruising, slalom, freeride and downhill. Cruising is simply used for transport. The other types are more extreme. Slalom requires riders to travel in between and around obstacles. Freeride is the most creative type, with riders performing tricks such as kickflips, cross steps and tiger claws. The most extreme type is downhill, which brings riders to high speeds. The world record for downhill speed on a longboard is 130 kilometres (80 miles) per hour.

SKATEBOARDING SUBCULTURE

Many skateboarders fell in love with the sport in the 1980s. But they felt like skateboarding didn't fit into mainstream sports. As a result, a **subculture** was created around extreme skateboarding. Today many skateboarders still follow this way of life.

subculture – a group of people who believe or behave differently from the main group within a culture

British Columbia, Canada's Britannia Classic features a freeride and race for longboarders competing in Canada.

CHAPTER 4

Mountainboarding

Extreme athletes are always looking for new, fun ways to test themselves. Mountainboarding is a good example of their creativity. Many love snowboarding, but snow is not always available. To solve this problem, mountainboarding was invented. Mountainboarding mixes aspects of skateboarding, snowboarding and even cycling. It can be done almost anywhere.

A mountainboard looks like a cross between a snowboard and a skateboard. Bindings secure the rider's feet to a long board that curves up at the ends, like a snowboard. Like a skateboard, the board has wheels mounted on the bottom. However, these are not average skateboard wheels. They are larger and stronger. This makes them good for all types of **terrain**. Some mountainboards even have motors for extra speed and power.

Unlike a snowboard or a skateboard, a mountainboard does not require any special weather or surface. It can travel over rocks, dirt, grass and other terrain, giving riders an "off-road" experience. The places a mountainboarder rides can be unpredictable. This is what makes the sport so exciting. The best mountainboarders can ride at speed and dodge obstacles in their path. They can also perform imaginative **freestyle** tricks.

terrain – the surface of the land
freestyle – a branch of a sport that focuses on tricks and jumps

Serbia holds a world championship for mountainboarding every year. The trail is 700 m (2,300 feet) long.

EXTREME FACT!

Riders have experimented with different mountainboard designs. They have used boards with two, three and four wheels.

CHAPTER 5

Extreme biking

Extreme bikers have taken their sport to the next level, with BMX and freestyle motocross (FMX).

BMX is not your average cycling sport. Special bikes are used for racing and tricks. High speeds, creative tricks and stunts, and lots of competition define BMX.

BMX was first developed around the 1970s. Children and teenagers in the United States fell in love with the speed and stunts of motocross. However, motocross requires expensive motorcycles. These young **pioneers** created their own version, using unpowered bikes on motocross tracks. BMX was born.

BMX bikes are small and light, to allow riders better control for racing and stunts. Bike designs can vary based on the riding style. In freestyle riding, competitors use their bikes to perform stunts. These bikes sometimes have **pegs** and no brakes. In BMX racing, bikes are as light as possible so that riders can reach top speeds.

pioneers – people who are the first to try new things

pegs – metal cylinders attached to the axles

BMX contests are held all over the world. In Portugal, riders like Sauro Agostinho compete in the DVS BMX Series.

FMX riders wear special gear, including a heavy-duty helmet, to protect them from injury.

Unlike BMX, FMX riders use motorbikes. Since they have extra power, motorbikes can be much more dangerous than BMX bikes.

The two types of FMX competitions are freestyle and big air. Freestyle was developed first. In freestyle motocross, riders perform routines involving different kinds of jumps. A routine can last anywhere from 90 seconds to several minutes.

Big air motocross gives riders the chance to take on the most extreme jumps in the sport. Riders launch their bikes off a dirt ramp and perform exhilarating stunts while airborne. In both freestyle and big air competitions, a panel of judges chooses the winner. Riders are scored based on style, difficulty of tricks and originality.

FMX tricks are some of the most dangerous in the world. Even their names are extreme. Popular FMX tricks include the superman, Hart attack, suicide can and double backflip. FMX riders also modify the length of ramps from time to time to do more extreme stunts, such as 540 spins.

EXTREME FACT!

In 2014, Josh Sheehan set an FMX world record by landing a triple backflip. No one had ever successfully done this before.

CHAPTER 6

Aggressive in·line skating

You might be familiar with rollerblading. This can be a fun activity for people of all ages. But there is also an extreme version. Skaters who pushed rollerblading to its limits created aggressive in-line skating.

The "aggressive" in aggressive in-line skating does not mean there is anger or violence involved. It simply means that this is a type of in-line skating that is fast-paced, challenging and truly hard-core. Skaters skate for show, performing all sorts of grinds, spins, jumps, slides and flips. This sport gives them room for endless creativity.

The skates used in aggressive in-line skating are designed to be tougher than average skates. The wheels are generally hard, so they can handle lots of wear and tear. The boots are built to support skaters' ankles during stunts.

Aggressive in-line skaters visit skateparks to practise their skills. Skate parks have equipment, such as halfpipes, that skaters can use to train. Aggressive in-line skaters use this equipment to practise challenging grinds and spins. They also love meeting other skaters at skateparks.

Obstacles offer opportunities for tricks. Skaters can perform tricks such as grinds on walls.

EXTREME FACT!

The best skates for aggressive in-line skating can be very expensive. Some cost more than £800!

CHAPTER 7

Parkour

Parkour is one of the most imaginative extreme land sports. There is no set location or equipment needed for parkour. It can be practised anywhere. The goal of this sport is to get from one place to another, regardless of obstacles in the way.

Parkour is often based on **efficiency** in terms of total distance travelled. People who practice parkour are called traceurs. They try to use obstacles like walls, gaps and railings to reach a certain place. A regular person would use stairs to get from the ground to a rooftop. But a traceur may scale the side of the building, use railings or ledges to gain height, or hop from wall to wall to reach their goal. In the process, they might also perform flips, rolls and other exciting moves.

Modern parkour comes from an old type of French military training. Extreme athletes **adapted** it to create a new sport. The basic movements of parkour are jumps, landings, vaults and wall manoeuvres. Traceurs who are just starting out will practise and master these moves first. Then they can begin to take on more challenging moves. Some traceurs even invent their own stunts. There are truly no limits for this creative extreme sport.

efficiency – the ability to do something well without wasted energy

adapt – change to be better suited for an environment

Traceurs see parkour as more than just a physical sport. They also use it to express themselves.

CHAPTER 8

Sand kiting

It might be hard to imagine sport practised on the hot sands of a desert. However, in the true spirit of extreme sports, riders created an activity to suit their surroundings. A board, a controllable kite and wind power are all a person needs to "surf" over the sand.

Sand kiting can be done on sand dunes, in deserts or even on the beach. Strong winds – some reaching more than 64 km (40 miles) per hour – allow sand kiters to perform huge jumps.

Of all the extreme land sports, sand kiting is one of the newest. People are still developing new sand kiting techniques and tricks. They often share their experiences in online videos.

One common element for new sand kiters is safety. No matter how extreme, athletes wear helmets in case of an accident. Even though sand looks soft, it can lead to a painful fall – just imagine falling on sandpaper!

Some people surf sand dunes without using a kite or wind power. This type of boarding is called sandboarding.

One of the most popular places to go sand kiting is in the vast deserts of Morocco.

EXTREME FACT!

A sandboarder called Josh Tenge holds the world record for the longest-distance backflip on a sandboard. His record is 14 m (44 feet, 10 in)! He set this record jumping off a dune in Sand Mountain, Nevada, USA, in 2000.

CHAPTER 9

Zorbing

Zorbing might be the strangest extreme land sport of all time. This sport was developed in New Zealand in the 1990s. In order to go zorbing, a person enters a large, clear plastic ball and rolls down a hill or track. The ride involves exhilarating rotations and bounces.

The plastic ball, known as a zorb, is actually one large ball with a slightly smaller ball inside. This allows the zorb to stay inflated with air. Some zorbs have harnesses to keep riders in place. Others are partially filled with water. This allows riders to slide around the ball as it moves.

Although some people go zorbing for fun, others take it to the extreme. The most extreme zorbers aim for the longest rides and the fastest speeds. The fastest zorber in the world, Keith Kolver, holds the record at 51.8 km (32.2 miles) per hour.

Extreme land sports are creative, challenging and always changing. They give adrenaline junkies the chance to make use of the natural environment in totally new ways.

EXTREME FACT!

In 2006, Steve Camp set the record for the greatest distance travelled by a zorb in a single roll at 570 m (1,871 feet).

Even though it is new and different, this wacky extreme sport is relatively safe, thanks to the zorb's design.

Glossary

adapt change to be better suited for an environment

descend to move from a higher place to a lower place

efficiency the ability to do something well without wasted energy

formation the way in which items, such as rocks, are arranged

freestyle a branch of a sport that focuses on tricks and jumps

friction device a mechanical piece of equipment that helps control a rope

pegs metal cylinders attached to the axles

pioneer people who are the first to try new things

subculture a group of people who believe or behave differently from the main group within a culture

summit the very top of a mountain; many summits are covered with snow

terrain the surface of the land

Find out more

Extreme Sports (The Wimp's Guide), Tracey Turner (Franklin Watts, 2013)

Freerunning Champion (How to Be a ...), James Nixon (Franklin Watts, 2015)

Inline Skating (Action Sports), John Hamilton (A&D Xtreme, 2014)

Rock Climbing (Adventure Sports), Stephanie Turnbull (Smart Apple Media, 2016)

Websites

http://teacher.scholastic.com/scholasticnews/indepth/
Skateboarding/articles/index.asp?article=history&topic=0

https://www.thebmc.co.uk/climb-outside-how-to-start-rock-
climbing-outdoors

http://www.kidzworld.com/article/6121-motocross-101

http://www.kidzworld.com/article/5802-free-running

Index